CW00417926

# THE LIFE & TIMES OF MARCO POLO

All quotations are taken from *The Travels of Marco Polo*, trans & introd. by Ronald Latham (Harmondsworth, 1958).

# THE LIFE & TIMES OF

# Marco Polo

BY
James Brown

SHOOTING STAR PRESS

This edition printed for, Shooting Star Press Inc, 230
Fifth Avenue, Suite 1212, New York, NY 10001

Shooting Star Press books are available at special discount
for bulk purchases for sales promotions, premiums, fund-
raising or educational use. Special editions or book
excerpts can also be created to specification. For details
contact – Special Sales Director, Shooting Star Press Inc.,
230 Fifth Avenue, Suite 1212, New York, NY 10001

This edition first published by Parragon Books
Produced by Magpie Books Ltd, 7 Kensington Church
Court, London W8 4SP
Copyright © Parragon Book Service Ltd 1994
Cover picture & illustrations courtesy of: Mary Evans
Picture Library; Christies Images.

ISBN 1 57335 040 0
A copy of the British Library Cataloguing in Publication
Data is available from the British Library.

Typeset by Hewer Text Composition Services, Edinburgh
Printed in Singapore by Printlink International Co.

# INTRODUCTION

Three flagstones from the door.

Two and a half flagstones.

Two.

He was watching the beam of sunlight that was streaming through the window-bars creep across the floor and then up the wall as the day wore on.

Time passed slowly in prison. The sun rose; the sun set. The shadows crept across the floor, up the wall, dimmed and vanished. Rustichello had seen many days like that – fourteen years of them. This was no place for a professional writer such as himself. He ought to be out in courts, currying favour, entertaining people, conjuring up wondrous worlds in the mind's eye.

However, things had got more interesting of late. The prison was filled to bursting point with Venetians – POWs from a recent sea-battle. Just another boring trade dispute. They could try telling stories to pass the time, he supposed. He glanced over at his cell-mate. No, maybe not. The other man looked altogether too down-to-earth for such an imaginative pastime. A very solid citizen; a hard-nosed merchant, Rustichello conjectured. Must be about forty-five. One of those tough, no-nonsense types. If he ever got talking, he'd probably bore you to sobs with commodity prices and trade news.

★   ★   ★

The middle-aged man whom Rustichello found himself in prison with in Genoa was indeed a merchant. But he was also in all probability the most widely travelled man of his day. He had seen things so astonishing that his fellow-countrymen suspected him of making most of them up. From the politically fractious Europe of the thirteenth century he had journeyed far to the East, where he had encountered what was arguably the greatest empire the world has ever seen. There he had served its ruler, Kubilai Khan, the Great Khan, for seventeen years.

Then he had returned home to Venice, and in the course of a dispute with Genoa had been made prisoner after a sea-battle, probably in 1298.

# TRAVELS OF THE ELDER POLOS

The merchant's name, Marco Polo, is now inextricably associated with the extraordinary tale of his travels, which he dictated to Rustichello in Genoa. But the immense journeys which have made him famous were not originally his idea. It all started with his father, Niccolo, and his uncle Maffeo. They set off in about 1260 on a trading journey, hoping to find new and profitable markets. They left little Marco,

who had been born in 1254, at home in
Venice with his mother. According to some
sources, Marco was not even born when his
father left. At any event, Niccolo would not
see his son again for nearly ten years.

In 1260 the brothers had got to Constantinople. Hoping for profit, they resolved to
cross the Black Sea to Sudak. The same hope
tempted them to go on, until they came to
the dominions of Barka Khan. They lingered
with him for a year, striking lucrative bar-
gains. Then fate took a hand. Hulagu, Khan
of the Levant, made war on Barka. The war
made travel back in the direction from which
the brothers had come impossible so, as
Marco later reported, they reflected, 'Since
we cannot return to Constantinople with
our wares, let us go on towards the east.
Then we can come back by a roundabout

route.' Their return journey was to prove exceptionally roundabout.

As they travelled they happened upon an emissary of Hulagu's on his way to visit Hulagu's brother, Kubilai, the Great Khan, The emissary had never seen Europeans before, and persuaded them to accompany him to the court of the Great Khan, in the hope that the Khan would be intrigued to meet them.

He was decisive about everything else, but in matters of religion the Great Khan hedged his bets. His attitude to religion was, approximately, the more the merrier. He took out a sort of spiritual insurance policy, arguing that since he could not be sure which was the true god, it was as well to honour all plausible candidates 'so that I may be sure of doing [honour] to him who is the greatest in heaven and the truest; and to him I pray for aid'.

Having welcomed the two brothers, the Khan questioned them about Europe (the Khan was always thirsty for knowledge – something which was to be the making of Marco Polo), and he entrusted them with a mission. The brothers had urged him to become a Christian, and so the Khan challenged them to go to the Pope and return with some sacred oil from the lamp in Christ's sepulchre in Jerusalem and a 'hundred men learned in the Christian religion', who would be able to prove the truth of Christianity.

The brothers' return journey was expedited within the Great Khan's territory by a gold

tablet he had given them, instructing his
subjects to render them every assistance.
Even so, it took them three years. But
longer delays were in store. They fetched
up in Christendom again in 1269 only to
find that the Pope had died. They consulted
Tedaldo of Piacenza, the Papal Legate to
Egypt, who advised them that there was
nothing for it but to wait for the election
of a new Pope. In the mean time the
brothers decided to go home, and so made
for Venice. It was just as well they did, for
the election of the new Pope was to take
another two years.

# FALSE STARTS

Niccolo returned home to find that his wife had died in his absence. The son who had been at most a toddler when he had last seen him (if indeed he had ever seen him) was now a teenager – virtually a young man. Young Marco's strength and maturity were soon to be put to the test. When after two years the Papal election was still not concluded, the brothers decided that they could keep the Great Khan waiting no longer. They set off eastwards once more, taking

Marco with them. They obtained some of the holy oil and consulted Tedaldo again. He furnished them with letters explaining to the Great Khan what had delayed the brothers and why they had not exactly fulfilled their mission. Thus prepared, they headed for the Tartar Empire.

They'd not gone far, however, when word reached them that Tedaldo himself had been elected Pope, and wanted them to turn back. So they returned to Acre in Palestine, received further letters from the man who was now Pope Gregory X, and also had two learned Dominican friars, Brother Nicholas and Brother William, added to their party. Two friars were a far cry from the hundred learned men the Khan asked for, but doubtless the Polos thought two would be better than none.

Marco Polo

The port in Venice

If so, they were mistaken. The party got as far as Ayas when it ran into more trouble: the Sultan of Egypt was invading Armenia. Whatever the spiritual qualities of the two Dominicans, they lacked physical courage. In alarm, they handed over to the Polos all the documents the Pope had entrusted to them and prevailed upon the Grand Master of the Templars to take them with him out of the war zone. The Polos carried on alone.

# TRAVELLING TO THE KHAN

The story of the travels on which the young Marco was now at last properly embarked, and which years later he was to tell to Rustichello in that Genoese prison, is as frustrating to read as it is fascinating. Although full of interest, one can glean from it only the most general notion of Marco Polo himself. The tale is told with few concessions to today's interest in personalities. Much of the work is organized primarily to convey information. Like the merchant that he was, Marco notes the main produce of most of the places he visits and their degrees of prosperity. Though the thread of the story of the great journey comes to the surface occasionally, it does not predominate. But, along with practical information, Marco includes any interesting stories he's picked up – some of them, as will be seen, quite fantastic. But he reports all as sober fact: griffins capable of flying off with an elephant in their talons share the same pages as details of the fabrics produced in each city, and local customs, and practical traveller's tips.

One can be sure of one thing about Marco Polo: he must have been tough. He would have needed to be to endure year after year in the saddle, or sometimes at sea, making his tortuous way out to the court of the Great

Khan, undertaking the missions the Khan entrusted to him, and then at last making a home-coming dogged by bad luck in the course of which many of his travelling companions died.

Marco gives the reader the occasional insight into the practical difficulties he encountered. Arriving in Hormuz on the Persian Gulf, he offers grimly believable details of the effect of the local diet on one's digestion, and then casts a warily experienced and critical eye over the local ships, which are untrustworthy because, instead of being nailed, they are 'stitched together with a thread made of coconut husks'. Even though the thread 'lasts remarkably well', Marco explains that it is 'a risky undertaking to sail in these ships. And you can take my word for it that many of them sink . . .'

Not surprisingly, the Polos turned inland from Hormuz. But other perils awaited them. 'Don't drink the local water' was valid advice then as now. Marco records that for three days after leaving Kerman (north of Hormuz) the only water to be found is 'brackish and green . . . Drink one drop of it and you void your bowels ten times over'. A little further on, beyond Kuh-banan, the water is almost as bad as before, except that Marco tells us one can just about use it for the animals, provided one follows his tip and tempts them to drink by mixing the foul water with flour.

Ill health must have been a constant danger under these circumstances. It was fortunate, then, that after contracting some disease, possibly from the water or maybe back in Hormuz, Marco arrived in Badakhshan. In this kingdom many of the cities were built on mountains, where 'the air is so pure and so salubrious that if a man living in the cities and houses built in the adjoining valleys falls sick of a fever, whether tertian, quartan, or hectic, he has only to go up into the mountains, and a few days rest will banish the malady and restore him to health. Messer Marco vouches for this from his own experience.' He must have been relieved to find such a curative atmosphere; according to one of the versions of the *Travels*, he had been ill for a year before regaining his health in the mountains of Badakhshan.

# MARCO'S TRAVELS: FACT OR FANTASY

This kind of detail about the condition of ships and the gut-wrenching effects of desert water fascinates because it is so realistic. Others are more bizarre, and even incredible. How much can one believe? The dividing line between personal experience and fanciful hearsay is sometimes hard to draw. For example, Marco notes that the area around the city of Kamadin is plagued by gangs of robbers called the Karaunas, who 'work an enchantment by diabolic art so that the day turns dark and no one can see more than a very short distance. This darkness they spread over an extent of seven days' journey . . . When they have brought on the darkness, they ride side by side, sometimes as many as 10,000 of them together . . .' This all sounds utterly unbelievable, but one is then told that 'Messer Marco himself narrowly evaded capture by these robbers in the darkness they had made. He escaped to a town called Kamasal; but many of his companions were taken captive and sold, and some put to death.' Though the account of the Karaunas darkness is exaggerated, it has been suggested that it may have been a phenomenon known as 'dry fog', created by fine dust being swirled in hot winds. Whatever it was, Marco obviously had a hair-raisingly narrow escape.

Early map of Europe and Asia

Marco Polo sets off on his travels

Later during the journey out, Marco tells of another phenomenon, which, like the magical darkness of the robbers, looks quite unbelievable at first, though one later wonders whether there is not some basis in fact for it. Marco is crossing the Desert of Lop, or, as we know it today, the Gobi Desert. He offers practical information about the availability of water, and notes the lack of wildlife. Then his recollections get stranger:

'When a man is riding by night through this desert and something happens to make him loiter and lose touch with his companions, by dropping asleep or for some other reason, and afterwards he wants to rejoin them, then he hears spirits talking in such a way that they seem to be his companions. Sometimes, indeed, they even hail him by name. Often these voices make him stray from the path, so that he never finds it again. And in this way many travellers have been lost and have perished. And sometimes in the night they are conscious of a noise like the clatter of a great cavalcade of riders away from the road; and, believing that these are some of their own company, they go where they hear the noise and, when day breaks, find they are victims of an illusion and in an awkward plight. And there are some who, in crossing this desert, have seen a host of men coming towards them and, suspecting that they were robbers, have taken flight; so, having left the beaten track and not knowing how to return to it, they have gone hopelessly astray. Yes, and even by daylight men hear these spirit voices, and often you fancy you are listening to the strains of many instruments, especially drums, and the clash of arms. For this reason bands of travellers make a point of keeping very close together. Before they go to sleep they set up a sign pointing in the direction in which they have to travel. And round the necks of all their beasts they fasten little bells, so that by listening to the sound they may prevent them from straying off the path.'

It's the sensible practicality of the last three sentences that makes one reconsider the plausibility of the description, which can be read as a vivid account of mirages and hallucinations induced by exhaustion and extreme heat.

But some of the tales Marco reports as hearsay are frankly fantastic. In 1225 the Caliph of Baghdad insisted that all the Christians in his city would either have to abandon their faith, or be put to death – or prove theirs the true faith by moving a mountain. The Christians prayed for the mountain to move, but to no effect, until an angel came to tell their bishop that they should persuade a certain shoemaker to pray for the mountain to move. This shoemaker was so holy a man that, on finding the sight of the ankle of a lady customer temptingly attractive, he promptly rebuked himself by putting the offending eye out with an awl. The bishop eventually persuaded the now one-eyed shoemaker to join them on the appointed day and beseech the mountain to shift, which it allegedly did, to the astonishment of the Caliph, who secretly became a Christian in consequence. Likewise, Marco reports tales of the legendary Christian ruler, Prester John, as if they were simple fact.

Some of the things Marco reports are not necessarily untrue, but are highly exotic –

violent or sexually charged, or both. The western stereotype of the East found early expression. One such thing is the story of the Old Man of the Mountain. If the phrase summons up an image of a benign and contemplative hermit, forget it. The old man in question was a power-crazed sheikh called Alaodin, who realized that one way to power was to annihilate his rivals. Accordingly, he ran a dedicated hit-squad which he motivated in a bizarre way.

In a valley he created a paradise on Earth: gardens, palaces, the lot. There flowed streams and fountains of wine, water, milk and honey. The permanent residents were a bevy of the most gorgeous and beguiling women.

There was only one way into the valley: through a well nigh impregnable castle.

24

Meanwhile in the outside world Alaodin kept his eyes peeled for likely recruits to his band of assassins. The chosen few would be drugged and carried into the valley of delights. They would awake to find themselves in the lap of luxury, surrounded by compliant women. They naturally assumed this really was paradise in the next world.

When a job came up, Alaodin would drug his chosen hit-man and have him deposited back outside. Alaodin had somehow managed to acquire a reputation for holiness, so that when he told the hapless assassin that the only way back to heavenly bliss involved killing so-and-so, the assassin would be motivated accordingly. Death ceased to be a consideration: the paradise he had tasted would be his again whether he died or not –

European traders in Levant

Rural life in Marco Polo's time

or so he believed. None whom the sheikh took against lived long.

Finally Hulagu, brother of the Great Khan, destroyed Alaodin, though he had to besiege the castle for three years to do it.

The story of the Old Man of the Mountain may be true – at root. But it has a shape as a story which may suggest that Rustichello, the professional story-teller, polished it up. But whatever parts of Marco's travels beggar belief, overall they clearly have some foundation in fact.

# LOCAL CUSTOMS: SEX AND MARRIAGE

As Marco travelled he was struck by the differences in customs and beliefs of the various peoples he encountered.* He is apt to dismiss the non-Christian religions he encountered with the phrase 'The people here are all idolaters'. Given the ham-fisted

* For the sake of convenience this section and the next deal with Marco's observations throughout the *Travels*, not just with the journey out to the Khan.

27

mess he makes of trying to explain the Buddhist concept of reincarnation, it is possibly as well that the details of other faiths seldom interest him. Such things were perhaps too abstract for him. But when it comes to the specific details of local customs and practices, Marco is a much keener observer.

Marriage customs and sexual mores attract particular attention. Marco does not give much away about himself, but there is a hint that his interest was not purely theoretical. He visited a district which he calls Tibet (actually a larger area than that which we now know as Tibet) on a mission for the Great Khan, and discovered a community that was very strictly against adultery, and equally strictly in favour of pre-marital sex. Indeed, the latter was virtually obligatory:

'Here there prevails a marriage custom of which I will tell you. It is such that no man would ever on any account take a virgin to wife. For they say that a woman is worthless unless she has had knowledge of many men. They argue that she must have displeased the gods, because if she enjoyed the favour of their idols then men would desire her and consort with her.'

The result of this is that travellers find that mothers bring their daughters along and offer them up. All they want in return is a trinket. The daughters collect the trinkets to show how many lovers they have had, and so attract a husband. However, once married they must be strictly faithful. As Marco coyly observes, 'Obviously the country is a fine one to visit for a lad from sixteen to twenty-four.'

Tibet wasn't the only place that furnished such opportunities. In the province of Pem, when a woman's husband had to go on a journey of more than three weeks, she would take another husband in his absence. Even more obliging were the people of Kamul, who 'give no thought to anything but making music, singing and dancing, and reading and writing according to their own usage, and taking great delight in the pleasures of the body'. When a stranger arrives at one of their homes, the husband promptly absents himself for a few days, leaving his wife to the visitor's pleasure. Their overlord, Mongu Khan, tried to forbid the custom, but the people of Kamul were so distressed that they petitioned him with a rich gift to let them return to their welcoming ways.

By contrast, the virgins of Cathay were required to observe strict chastity. Their virginity would be tested on their marriage, and they were so wary of failing to pass the test that they 'always walk so daintily that they never advance one foot more than a finger's breadth beyond the other, since physical integrity is often destroyed by a wanton gait'. What with their modesty, their quietness and their deference to their elders, the virgins of Cathay sound sadly downtrodden.

# LOCAL CUSTOMS: DEATH

Of less immediate interest to the traveller were the various burial and funerary customs Marco encountered. The people of Sa-chau would only cremate their dead at the exact time specified by their astrologers. This could be up to six months after death. So they embalm the body, and seal it in an elaborately decorated coffin. Meanwhile, because the deceased is still theoretically alive, they continue to serve him or her meals, which are set in front of the coffin.

The astrologers can even prescribe how the coffin should be carried out of the house, occasionally having a wall demolished to avoid using an unlucky door.

The death rituals of Sa-chau were merely dotty; but those surrounding the funeral of a Great Khan were terrifying. The Great Khans, descendants of the mighty Chinghiz (Genghis), are laid to rest on Mount Altai:

'And here is a remarkable fact: when the body of a Great Khan is being carried to this mountain – be it forty days' journey or more or less – all those who are encountered along the route by which the body is being conveyed are put to the sword by attendants who are escorting it. 'Go,' they cry, 'and serve your lord in the next world.' . . . It is a fact that, when Mongu Khan died, more than 20,000 men were put to death, having encountered his body on the way to burial.'

Scarcely less gruesome, though less wantonly destructive, were the eating habits of the *Bakhshi*, the Khan's enchanters, who could allegedly control the weather for him. Marco notes disparagingly that they really perform their magic by consorting with the devil, and are habitually in a state of filth and squalor. 'When a man is condemned to die and is put to death by the authorities, they take the body and cook and eat it. But, if anyone dies a natural death, they would never think of eating him.'

Somewhat like the Khan, when the King of one of the kingdoms of Maabar died, his barons cast themselves onto his funeral pyre to join him in the next world. They must sometimes have wished that they could swop over to the custom of the people of Manzi. The latter would accompany any great man to his funeral pyre, but once there were content merely to incinerate paper effigies of slaves, horses and camels.

By contrast, the Tartar way of dealing with the death of a child was poignant and constructive. A man whose young son has died will seek out a family that has lost a daughter of the same age, and they will arrange a marriage between the deceased. They then burn the contract 'and declare that the smoke that rises into the air goes to their children in the other world and that they get wind of it and regard themselves as husband and wife'. The two families then

The Polo brothers leave Constantinople

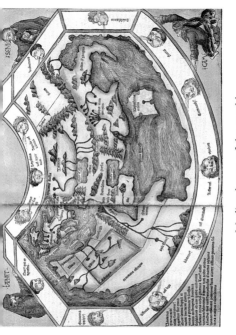

Medieval map of the world

hold a great wedding feast, and bind themselves to each other as kinsfolk, just as if their children really had been married.

# THE GREAT KHAN

Finally, after being on the road for three and a half years, the Polo brothers and young Marco drew near to Kubilai Khan himself. They must have felt apprehensive. Far from bringing a hundred learned Christians as requested, thanks to the vanishing act of Brothers William and Nicholas, they were bringing just themselves. And they had taken a long time over it – eight years.

The Khan got wind of their approach and had them met while still forty days' journey away. When they eventually presented themselves to the Great Khan, they found him in the city of Kemenfu, surrounded by 'a very great company of barons'. The Khan was delighted to receive the holy oil and letters from the Pope. If he was irked at the absence of learned friars, he seems to have been diplomatic enough not to mention it. Perhaps in nervous enthusiasm, when Niccolo introduced Marco to the Khan he presented him as 'my son, and your liegeman'. For the next seventeen years Marco would indeed be in the Khan's service.

Everything about the Great Khan was big. He ruled the biggest empire in the world and everything else about his life was to scale. As Marco insists, 'everyone should know that this Great Khan is the mightiest man, whether in respect of subjects or of territory or of treasure, who is in the world today or who ever has been'.

His palace in Khan-balik 'is the largest that was ever seen', its interior walls 'all covered with gold and silver and decorated with pictures of dragons and birds and horsemen and various breeds of beasts and scenes of battle'. The great hall could seat 6,000 for a feast. As if one such palace was not enough, the Great Khan had a pair of green palaces in the grounds, one for himself and 'another one . . . just like his own, and no whit inferior' for his successor. Within the extensive palace grounds roamed white harts, musk-deer, roebuck, stags and squirrels. Many species of fish swam in specially constructed lakes, on which paddled swans

Marco Polo pictured in the *Travels*

Marco Polo travels through China

and waterfowl. On a mound to the north of the palace the Khan kept his tree collection. Elephants carried the best trees in his domains, irrespective of their size, to be replanted here. Just in case the mound was not impressive enough, instead of grass, the Khan had the space between the trees covered with brilliant, green lapis lazuli.

In this epic setting the Khan lived for just three months each year.

During the summer he lived in another palace, Shang-tu, or as Coleridge's poem has it, Xanadu. It was here that the Khan kept a portable palace of canes, which could be dismantled and re-erected as he wished.

Just in case anyone failed to notice that the Khan was the most powerful man in the world, he had a personal bodyguard of 12,000 men, working in shifts of 3,000. Everything about him and his government smacked of military precision. This was even true of his pastimes. His principal huntsmen were two noble brothers, Bayan and Mingan. Each had command of 10,000 men and 5,000 hounds. There was another establishment to look to the Khan's 5,000 hawks. Hunting with the Khan was more like conducting a military campaign than having a day out. This was especially true when he set off each spring to travel from his winter quarters to the ocean, hawking as he went. The Khan would travel in a sort of mobile hunting-lodge carried on the backs of four elephants, with a special trap in the roof so that he could loose his gerfalcons on their prey without stirring from his couch.

Even the Khan's sex life was regimented. Every two years he used to send representatives to the province of Kungurat, noted for the beauty of its people, and they would select four or five hundred concubines rather as if they were recruiting for a crack regiment.

'This is how the selection is made. When the emissaries arrive, they summon to their presence all the maidens of the province. And there valuers are deputed for the task. After inspecting and surveying every girl feature by feature, her hair, her face, her eyebrows, her mouth, her lips and every other feature, to see whether they are well-formed and in harmony with her person, the valuers award to some a score of sixteen marks, to others seventeen, eighteen, or twenty, more or less according to the degree of their beauty. And, if the Great Khan has ordered them to bring him all who score twenty marks, or perhaps twenty-one, according to the number ordered, these are duly brought.'

At this point the whole process was repeated according to more exacting standards, including tests to make sure that they were virgins and did not snore. Finally the successful few joined teams of six who ministered to the Khan in relay. This was in addition to his four wives, each of whom boasted a household of 10,000.

Even the prostitutes of Khan-balik were run like an army. There were apparently 20,000 of them. 'They have a captain general, and there are chiefs of hundreds and thousands responsible to the captain'. In a manner of which many a latter-day madam might have approved, they paid their taxes kind by providing free entertainment for the Khan's official visitors.

# THE KHAN'S EMPIRE

The Khan was a man of immense curiosity about the world in general, and about the substantial part of it that he ruled in particular. This was the making of Marco. He picked up several of the local languages, and could write four of them. Duly impressed, the Khan entrusted him with missions. Marco had observed that the Khan liked to hear a general report on local customs and conditions from his emissaries, in addition to an account of

Chinese statesman in ceremonial dress

Kubilai Khan goes into battle

the business he had entrusted to them, castigating those who could not furnish such reports as 'dolts and dunces'. So Marco took care to note everything of interest while on his mission, and so delighted the Khan on his return that he won high praise and a position of trust.

However, the Great Khan was no closet intellectual. The empire he ruled was largely won by conquest and maintained by military domination. He stood at the head of a complex bureaucracy of delegated power, but in the end it was the army that the Tartar Empire depended on. The Khan himself had been a shrewd general in his younger days, on one occasion skilfully launching a surprise attack on a stronger rebel army, led by Nayan. Nayan was of royal blood, which by custom could not be spilt – so after the victory the Khan had him wrapped in a carpet and clubbed to death.

Most of the Khan's armies were led by his generals. They were all organized in multiples of ten. The officers were graded according to whether they commanded 100, 1,000, 10,000 or 100,000 men. Each had a special tablet from the Khan conferring his authority. Officers could move both up and down the chain of command, depending on performance. And such was the nature of the Tartar Empire that there was plenty of opportunity to perform.

Marco gives the impression that on the whole the Tartar Empire was a model of efficiency and irresistible power, but just occasionally the Khan's system of delegated power broke down. There was the evil

Saracen, Ahmad, who completely won the Khan's trust, and then lined his own pockets, had his opponents executed, and took any woman he wanted, bribing and threatening her family into compliance. He was a governor in Cathay. Eventually the Cathayans were driven to revolt. They duped Ahmad into thinking that Chinghiz, the Khan's son, had arrived and wished to see him. Ahmad was beheaded as soon as he entered the throne room. His crimes came to light in the wake of the ruthless suppression of the revolt. Learning of Ahmad's ill-gotten gains, the Khan appropriated his treasure for himself.

Corruption wasn't the only problem that could disrupt the Tartar Empire. Occasionally incompetence played its part, as in the ill-fated Tartar invasion of Japan. The

Khan sent a force under two lords, Aba-
kan and Vonsamchin, against the island.
Unfortunately the two commanders were
feuding with each other, with the result
that in a gale their refusal to co-operate
with each other cost them so many ships
that they had to leave 30,000 men behind
on an island, while they went home with
the main body of the army. These 30,000
were finer men than their commanders.
The Japanese, thinking themselves safe and
seeing a large number of the enemy
marooned and apparently at their mercy,
set sail to capture them. The 30,000
Tartars prudently withdrew to the other
side of the island, then sneaked round
unseen to the enemy fleet and sailed in
it back to Japan, where they seized the
capital. In due course the Japanese army
managed to return and for seven months

laid siege to the Khan's men, who were finally obliged to surrender on honourable terms.

When the generals' incompetence came to light the Khan was livid. One of them was executed immediately, the other sent to die slowly on the island of Zorza, where his hands were bound in fresh buffalo hide, which shrank as it dried. This was painful, and also rendered the victim helpless, unable to catch or prepare food. He would crawl about on his belly for a time, before succumbing to hunger or exhaustion.

Normally the Tartar armies were frighteningly efficient and rigorously disciplined. A Tartar army on the move was difficult to surprise, for it was surrounded by a couple of hundred scouts who were many miles from the main force. In action they were even more formidable. One of their favourite tactics was to pretend to retreat – something which required the most precise discipline:

'When they are pursued and take to flight, they fight as well and as effectively as when they are face to face with the enemy. When they are fleeing at top speed, they twist round with their bows and let fly their arrows to such good purpose that they kill the horses of the enemy and the riders too. When the enemy thinks he has routed and crushed them, then he is lost; for he finds his horses killed and not a few of his men. As soon as the Tartars decide that they have killed enough of the pursuing horses and horsemen, they wheel round and attack and acquit themselves so well and courageously that they gain a complete victory.'

Marco Polo encountered many colourful character on his travels

Travellers arriving at a palace in China

They were also cool under attack. Marco tells of their first encounter with elephants in 1272. Their horses were so alarmed that the Tartar cavalry could not get into battle. As if that wasn't bad enough, they were outnumbered 40,000 to 12,000. They didn't panic. Taking cover in a wood, they dealt with the elephants with their bows and arrows, then remounted and beat the rest of the army.

But however efficient the Tartars were as soldiers, the cause for which they fought did not always bear scrutiny. Their dependence on force meant that they were prone to resort to violence to settle their differences. Marco records that the Great Khan and his nephew Kaidu fought many battles with each other. The culture of violence extended to Kaidu's daughter, Aiyaruk. She was so strong as to be a formidable warrior in her own right. Her father gave her the unusual privilege of choosing her own husband. She sent out a challenge: the man who would marry her had to beat her first. Many tried and failed. The price exacted from failed suitors was 100 horses; Aiyaruk accumulated 10,000 horses. Then there came the son of a mighty king, never beaten in combat. He was so confident he brought 1,000 horses. Kaidu was so taken with him that he intimated to his daughter that she might let her opponent win. But Aiyaruk was a true Tartar and was having none of it: she added another 1,000 horses to her tally.

Apart from invasion and feuding, the main function of the army was to keep the Khan's subjects in their place. Not everyone was as enthralled by the Khan as Marco was. For example, '. . . in all the province of Cathay

and Manzi and all the rest of his dominions
there are many disaffected and disloyal subjects who, if they had the chance, would
rebel against their lord'.

# MARCO POLO IN THE SERVICE OF THE KHAN

This was the empire in which Marco Polo served for seventeen years, though in what precise capacity it is hard to know. The *Travels* claim that he was governor of Yang-chau for three years. But the Chinese records have survived and do not bear him out. However, he does seem to have travelled extensively in the Khan's service. One version of the *Travels* records that he was sent on a mission to India, but for the most part

Marco Polo's home in Venice

Coin showing head of Marco Polo

they record little of the specific tasks with which he was entrusted.

Whatever they were, as he went about them Marco continued to accumulate information, quaint and horrifying, mundane and fantastic. He tells of various kinds of magic. The Khan's enchanters could supposedly control the weather and make cups fly through the air to the Khan's hand. In the kingdom of Dagroian there were astrologers who were believed in so completely that if they predicted a fatal outcome for a patient suffering from some ailment, the patient's relatives would send for men entrusted with putting such folk to death. Under the circumstances there was not much chance of the astrologers ever being proved wrong.

Marco struggles to describe the exotic crea-
tures he has encountered to his European
readers. Crocodiles are described as 'huge
snakes and serpents' up to ten paces long,
equipped with claws, teeth and bulging eyes.
Gradually the image familiar to every visitor
to a zoo or to anyone who's seen a Tarzan
film materializes. One is at first more startled
by his claim to have seen 'plenty of unicorns'
– until one reads his description of them as
being about the size of an elephant, with feet
like an elephant's and the habit of carrying
their heads lowered, and one realizes that he
must be talking about rhinoceroses.

There is the expected handful of utterly
bizarre second-hand reports. Marco claims
that in the kingdom of the Lambri there are
men with tails the size of dogs', while on the
island of Andaman he says that there are men

'who have heads like dogs, and teeth and eyes like dogs' and are ferociously cruel. More credible, but equally repellent, are the mountain people of Ferlec who eat human flesh, and whose haphazard religious sense leads them to worship 'whatever they see first when they wake in the morning'. Or then again there is the community whose men live on one island, while the women live on another.

But perhaps the most impressive part of this phase of the *Travels* is also believable: Marco's description of the great Chinese city of Kinsai. Like Marco's native Venice, it was a city built on water, but on an incomparably larger scale. There was a lake on one side, a river on the other, and innumerable waterways between, all criss-crossed by some 12,000 bridges. Basing his estimate on tax returns, Marco put the total number of households at about 1,600,000.

Kinsai was a massive trading centre. The craftsmen of Kinsai were organized into twelve guilds, each of which was said to have some 12,000 workshops. But Kinsai was more than just a trading centre. It was a place of immense beauty, where lives of elegance and leisure were not the sole preserve of the great. In the middle of the lake were two islands, and on each of these islands was a luxurious palace. These were available to anyone who wished to hold a celebration. Indeed the whole lake served the citizens' appetite for gracious pleasure, for when they were not feasting on the islands, they could go partying on beautifully painted pleasure-boats.

The social organization of the city seems to have matched its commerce and its pleasures. Well-endowed hospitals provided a form of health service-cum-social security, not only curing the sick, but seeing to it they got back to work once cured. Kinsai also boasted an emergency fire service.

Only one shadow hung over the lives of the people of Kinsai: their subjugation to the Great Khan. This they resented. But as Marco explains, their indulgent life-style had been their undoing. Their last native king, Facfur, lost sight of his military responsibilities – a dangerous thing to do when the Great Khan was your neighbour.

# THE JOURNEY HOME

The desire to see Venice again grew upon the Polos. But if the empire of the Great Khan was hard to get into, it was even harder to get out of. The Great Khan liked the Polos, especially Marco. He did not wish to see them leave, and he was not a man whose wishes could be taken lightly. And there were also massive practical difficulties.

At last an opportunity arose. Bulagan, the beloved wife of Arghun, Khan of the Levant, died, stipulating that Arghun's next wife should be another of her family. Arghun sent three ambassadors to the Great Khan to find a suitable bride. The Great Khan obliged by entrusting the seventeen-year – old Lady Kokachin to them, and sending them on their way. Eight months into the return journey they ran into a war. Their route blocked, they had to return to the Great Khan.

When the ambassadors reappeared, Marco had just returned from a mission to India. Along with his uncles, he so impressed the ambassadors that they asked them to join Kokachin's escort in the attempt to get back to Persia by sea. The Polos saw their chance. Once again they sought the Khan's leave to go, and this time it was granted.

Having had his consent wrung from him, the Khan was generous. He gave them a fleet of fourteen ships, supplies for two years, and passport-tablets to guarantee their free passage through his territories. He also gave them letters for the Pope and the Kings of Europe. The Polos took their leave of the Great Khan and set sail for Persia. They would never see him again.

The Polos and Arghun's three ambassadors led a formidable company. Excluding the sailors, it numbered 600. Things went horribly wrong. Marco is frustratingly vague about exactly what happened, but of the 600, only eighteen survived, and two of the ambassadors perished as well.

However, Marco does give some indication of the kind of dangers that beset travellers in those seas. It might have been on this journey that he found himself stranded for five months in what he calls Java (i.e. Sumatra), sheltering inside a makeshift stockade and waiting for the weather to break, while cannibals prowled outside.

These seas were also infested with pirates who were as efficient as they were ruthless. They would sail in formation with five miles between each vessel, so that a fleet of about twenty could comb a hundred-mile stretch of sea for prey, while remaining in touch with each other. These pirates searched their victims thoroughly. They would make them drink a mixture of tamarind and sea-water to induce vomiting. The vomit they would then carefully sift for concealed gems. The pirates even had a regular base, courtesy of the king of Thana, who, to Marco's outrage, let them operate from his kingdom in return for all the horses they captured.

If they avoided being robbed at sea, they might still have been plundered on land. The rapacious people of the kingdom of Ely used to seize any vessel that happened up their estuary, on the dubious grounds that it was a gift from the gods.

For whatever reason, it was a sadly depleted party that arrived in Persia. Nor were their problems over. In their absence Arghun had died, and been succeeded by his brother, Kaikhatu. So they now had a bride, but no groom. After consulting with Kaikhatu, it was decided that Kokachin should marry Arghun's son, Ghazan. But he was out guarding the borders, so that meant another journey. Understandably, the Polos ran out of steam at this point; they stayed in Persia for nine months.

Maybe they were waiting for good weather. Maybe they were just tired. Their friendship with Kokachin may have contributed to their reluctance to move on. They had been through a lot together, and she had come to regard them as surrogate fathers. When finally they 'left her to go to their own country, she wept for grief at their going'. This was not their only sorrow, for at some point on the way home they heard of the death of the Great Khan. Even if they ever wanted to, it would be impossible to return to the East now their patron and protector was dead.

# HOME COMING

They got back to Venice in 1295. They had been away for nearly twenty-five years. When they knocked at the door of Ca' Polo, no one recognized them in their strange, Eastern clothes. It is said that they only established their identity in the end by holding a great banquet. For each course, they appeared in robes that got more and more sumptuous. Finally they brought in their shabby travelling clothes, and ripped open the seams to reveal a fortune in gems.

This may be fanciful, but they did not return empty-handed. A fourteenth-century inventory of the Doge's possessions records gifts from Kubilai Khan, which must have been sent with the Polos.

Little is known of the remainder of Marco's life. In 1298 the long-running rivalry between Venice and Genoa escalated so far that a sea-battle was fought off Curzola. Venice lost ships, and 7,000 Venetian prisoners were hauled off to Genoa to be ransomed or to rot – among them Marco Polo, who had fitted out and commanded one of the galleys.

While in prison, Marco started reminiscing about his Eastern experiences. This proved such a draw that Genoese society flocked to the prison to hear of his travels and of the Great Khan. In the end, Marco got so bored repeating the same stories that he was persuaded to write them down. He managed to have his notes sent from Venice – many of them probably made for the edification of the Great Khan himself. He also found himself a ghost-writer. In the same prison languished Rustichello, a writer of romances from Pisa, who had probably been incarcerated since 1284.

Marco Polo went home in May the following year. Thereafter his name figures in a few routine lawsuits as he went about his business: bailing out a wine smuggler in 1305; suing an agent for money owed on a consignment of musk in 1311; arguing about a party-wall in 1323. In 1324 he died. His will refers to his wife, Donata, and their three daughters, Fantina, Bellela and Moreta. One wonders how much he told his wife of what he had got up to in the exotic East.

By 1305 he had acquired a nickname: 'Il Milione'. This was possibly a sly jab at the implausibly huge scale of everything he had described in the East. But to his last breath Marco Polo stuck to his story. It is said that on his death-bed the sceptics pressed him to admit that much of the *Travels* was made up. His defiant reply was that he had not told *one half* of what he had really seen.

# LIFE AND TIMES

Julius Caesar
Hitler
Monet
Van Gogh
Beethoven
Mozart
Mother Teresa
Florence Nightingale
Anne Frank
Napoleon

## LIFE AND TIMES

JFK
Martin Luther King
Marco Polo
Christopher Columbus
Stalin
William Shakespeare
Oscar Wilde
Castro
Gandhi
Einstein

# FURTHER MINI SERIES
## INCLUDE

## THEY DIED TOO YOUNG

Elvis
James Dean
Buddy Holly
Jimi Hendrix
Sid Vicious
Marc Bolan
Ayrton Senna
Marilyn Monroe
Jim Morrison

# THEY DIED TOO YOUNG

Malcolm X
Kurt Cobain
River Phoenix
John Lennon
Glenn Miller
Isadora Duncan
Rudolph Valentino
Freddie Mercury
Bob Marley

# FURTHER MINI SERIES INCLUDE

## ILLUSTRATED POETS

Robert Burns
Shakespeare
Oscar Wilde
Emily Dickinson
Christina Rossetti
Shakespeare's Love Sonnets